the

paperclip

test

the
paperclip
test

mario gmür

translated by
sally-ann spencer

◪ SQUARE PEG

1 3 5 7 9 10 8 6 4 2

Square Peg, an imprint of Vintage,
20 Vauxhall Bridge Road,
London SW1V 2SA

Square Peg is part of the Penguin Random House group of companies
whose addresses can be found at global.penguinrandomhouse.com.

 Penguin
Random House
UK

Copyright © Mario Gmür 2016
Translation copyright © Sally-Ann Spencer 2016
Photographs © Zoltan Gabor

Mario Gmür has asserted his right to be identified as the author of this
Work in accordance with the Copyright, Designs and Patents Act 1988

First published by Square Peg in 2016
www.vintage-books.co.uk

A CIP catalogue record for this book is available from the British Library
ISBN 9781910931004
Printed and bound in China by C&C Offset Printing Co., Ltd

Set in ITC Avant Garde Gothic
Designed by Kris Potter

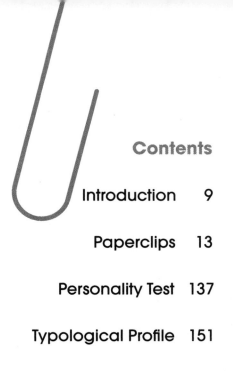

Contents

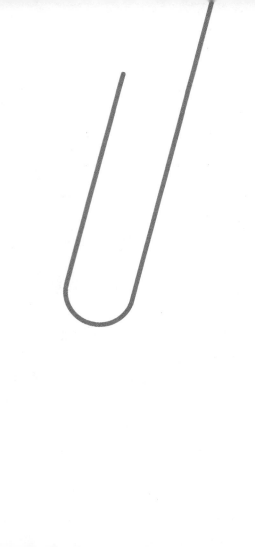

We all do it. Just check the bin
beside your desk ...

Fiddling with paperclips is a basic human impulse. There is something about these handy bits of metal that compels us to pick them up and bend them out of shape. We all do it. You don't believe me? Just check the bin beside your desk. You might be surprised by the number of misshapen paperclips inside it, but you shouldn't be. Like so much of what we do in life, we bend paperclips without really thinking.

At my clinic in Zurich, I usually sit opposite my patients at my desk. And as on every well-organised desk, there's a stash of paperclips in a little pot. Mine seems to be especially inviting as I realised that in the course of a session, a patient would always dip into the pot, pick up a paperclip, start to fiddle with it and – as if it were the most normal thing in the world – begin bending it out of shape. When the consultation was over, they would leave the paperclip on my desk or drop it in the bin on the way out. At some point, I decided to gather them up and save them.

After that it was a short leap to this book. I had the paperclips photographed by Zoltan Gabor and I used the images to develop a psychological test. It's designed so that anyone can use it. The test provides you with a profile that matches your personality – or describes the type of person you'd *like to be* – and it can even reveal unconscious character traits. It's not a test that should be taken too seriously, but my many guinea pigs' results have shown that it comes astonishingly close to the mark. If you want to learn more about yourself, this test is for you. What you have here is therefore a book of photographs, an introduction to psychology and a personality test all in one.

For the results of the test to be as unbiased and accurate as possible, I recommend not reading the descriptions of the different paperclips in advance. The results of the test won't decode your character once and for all – it can reflect your real personality or perhaps an idealised version of yourself; it may be a little too positive or too negative. Most importantly, I hope the test will prompt an interest in psychology and will help you to reflect on yourself, your quirks and personality traits. Afterwards, if you read the descriptions for all sixty paperclips, you'll be at least halfway to a psychology degree and you'll know a great deal more about people.

If you'd like extra copies of the test sheet, you can find it online at www.thepapercliptest.com. And one final thing to add: the names of the paperclips (see Paperclip Index on p. 205) relate to them as works of art and not to you, the test-subject. Now turn to p. 137 to get started.

paperclips

Fiddling with paperclips is a basic human impulse.

1

You possess healthy amounts of ambition
and drive. You are forward-looking and
believe in progress, but to this end you
are neither fanatical nor narrow-minded.
You are committed to the common good
and avoid competition with others;
however, you still like to be among the
key players. You are happiest when you
are leading the way or promoting
innovation, whether as a supplier of ideas,
encouragement or sponsorship. Always
open to new perspectives and suggestions,
you are intellectually curious. You listen to
opposing arguments without prejudice
and are generous in your acceptance
of different opinions, but you pursue your
convictions with determination.

2

You take things slowly, yet you always get there bang on time. Even before you do, your presence is tangible, because others anticipate your arrival, often impatiently. You succeed in getting what you want without overruling those around you or blocking their way. While others race blindly for the finish, you profit from taking your time and noticing what they miss. Your motto is the 'slower the better', and you are mindful that the higher you climb, the further you have to fall.

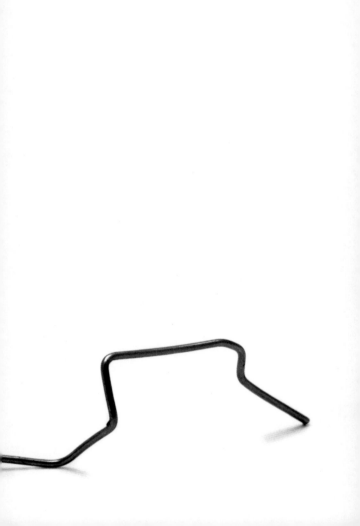

3

Passionate and sensuous, you love to be seduced. Leaping elegantly into the arms of temptation, you excel in the art of surrender. Life is a constant honeymoon: you refuse to be troubled by the mundane trials of everyday living. While others battle bureaucracy or society's expectations, you aren't thrown off your quest for indulgence. You trust your intuition and your brilliance. Duty and delight, gravity and gaiety exist for you in happy, mostly problem-free, symbiosis.

4

You like to shock, provoke and dumbfound: at times really go to town. You would be happier playing a drum kit than a harp. Ever the *enfant terrible*, your tomfoolery commands the full attention of your public. You're not picky: you rarely turn down material for your antics, and you seize any opportunity to perform. In the playground, at least, you are king.

5

You avoid the limelight but you love nothing more than a drama. You sit quietly at the back, biding your time. Then when no one expects it, you wrest control with a sudden rush of energy, like a volcano waking from its slumber and spewing magma for miles around. You have the potential to light a fire, then book yourself a front-row seat to watch the world burn.

6

You are an upright person in every sense
of the word: you stand tall and have
nothing to hide. You walk through life
with your head held high, but you never
seem stuck-up or condescending.
You are thoughtful and reflective,
but you tend towards complacency.
You value directness and want the world
to be straightforward. People often
come to you for advice. You wear your
largesse with modesty.

7

Naturally gifted, you achieve solid and sometimes exceptional results. Modesty prevents you from drawing attention to your successes, although secretly you hope to be praised. At the same time, you are sensitive to criticism, tending to back away to nurse your ego rather than admit to being hurt. But this behaviour may sabotage your chances of advancement and damage your self-esteem.

8

Appearances and presentation matter
to you. You find yourself drawn to
interesting and attractive objects; you
might photograph them. You also like to
pose, and you can be somewhat showy.
You prefer to let pictures do the talking
than waste your time on words. Sometimes
you block the way just for the fun of it.
In such cases, you accept your lot, alone,
out in the cold like a solitary guard.
Your goals in life are unambitious and
you are generally stoical. You accept
the status quo and make no particular
effort to generate change.

9

You do not aspire to reach the top. You have no high-flying career plans or grand ideas: you work hard to maintain average results. Middle of the field is your comfort zone, you do not sprint ahead to lead the pack, nor do you allow yourself to fall behind. You see no reason to subordinate yourself to others. In life, you cultivate a healthy minimalism. You are more likely to sign up for a sporting challenge than be co-opted for ambitious social or intellectual undertakings.

10

Stability and roots are more important to you than status or professional success. Things do not have to be big or bold for you to appreciate them. You favour quirky charm over pompous sophistication. You are not easily impressed or overawed, and it is not in your nature to be elitist: you give a fair chance to any endeavour that is serious and honest. Small creatures bring out your protective instincts. Family is your refuge.

11

You seem honest, open, innocent,
somewhat naïve and give the
impression of being helpful. You have
a gift for unobtrusively observing others:
then, in a flash, you have emptied
their pockets and made your escape.
You are adaptable and adroit and
are capable of putting your morally
dubious qualities to more public-spirited
use. You would make an excellent spy.

12

You are an inquisitive and patient observer,
whether as an astronomer, sociologist,
birdwatcher or simply in your day-to-day
affairs. Instinctively you put every event and
process under the microscope. Allowing
your mind and senses to remain open, you
broaden your knowledge and horizons as
you examine your surroundings in a leisurely
and roundabout manner. You are happy
to pursue your investigations away from
the action. You set your own pace and
resist the tyranny of speed.

13

You live by the motto 'if it ain't broke, don't fix it'. Down to earth and unpretentious, you are sceptical about anything fancy or high-flown, including most of modern life. Old-fashioned handiwork is what you know and love. The marvels of the natural world mean more to you than intellectual fireworks. You focus on the essentials and refuse to be dazzled by technology. The colours of the rainbow shine more brightly for you than the neon lights of Broadway.

14

The roots may not run deep, but you have your feet firmly on the ground and you are emotionally robust. You do not allow yourself to make mistakes and you refuse to be intimidated: it is not in your nature to flee. You pre-empt attacks by going on the defensive, which means no one really tries to take you on. You have the skill of an archer as well as the strength to wield a sword. You are seldom thrown off balance or taken unawares.

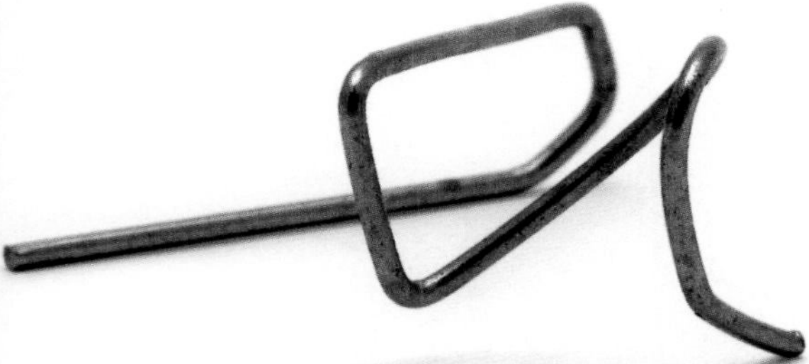

15

You are generally indecisive, you dislike confrontation, and for every step forward you take two steps back. Rather than rejoice at nearing your destination, you fret about what you may have forgotten along the way. You are risk averse, never daring to go out on a limb, and you weigh up every decision a hundred times over. Even though you have no shortage of energy you can be tiresome: you never do anything without worrying about what could go wrong.

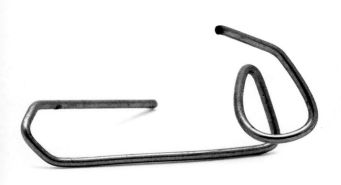

16

You claim every millimetre of space
that belongs to you. Wary of possible
incursions, you are constantly on guard.
Your obsessive vigilance saps the energy
you need to be creative. Despite your
formidable presence, you seldom initiate
anything or get concrete results. People
will remember you as a fortress that stood
staunch and unassailable in the face
of a self-inflicted siege.

17

You have a bright, welcoming personality and a cheerful outlook on life. People warm to you immediately and often fall under your magic spell, but their faith in you can lead to misunderstandings and land you in trouble. If this happens, you have ample inner space into which you retreat, enjoying the luxury of a private hideaway where you can be as colourful and dazzling as you like as you prepare your next conjuring trick.

18

You may experience setbacks, but not even total defeat will keep you down. You jump right back on your feet and throw yourself into battle again, attacking from new angles until your comeback is complete. No matter how many times your king is captured, you are ready for another match. In your eyes, surrender is worse than treason. You are a force to be reckoned with.

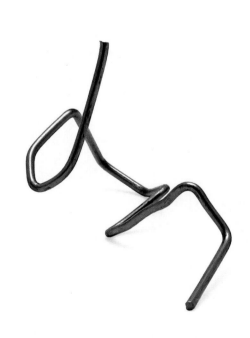

19

A well-balanced person, you are at
peace with yourself and your surroundings.
Your common sense leads you to avoid
extremes. When confronted with a problem,
you take the most straightforward
approach and resolve it in good time.
You never fuss, cause tension or polarise
opinions: people accept you. There is no
need to prove yourself: you inspire trust.

20

You have reached rock bottom. You gaze up wistfully at others and they feel compassion for you. Without the occasional handout you would struggle to survive. You manage to pull through and get there in the end, notwithstanding the odd setback. Despite your obsequiousness, you are respected for persevering and never losing hope. Some people even see you as a role model for those whom fate has dealt a cruel hand.

21

Moving forward in your own time,
you see no reason to rush. You like to take
breathers, refusing to be harried. You relish
the moment and seldom get bored or
worked up about things. You are happy
to stay in one place and enjoy the view,
or to return to familiar haunts yet never
have the paralysing sensation of going
round in circles. Even though in the prime
of youth, the fast lane is not for you.
You've opted for early retirement and
are content to watch the sun rising and
setting every day.

22

You feel unsure of yourself – mainly because of your present situation rather than any inherent self-doubt. Perhaps you are on the rebound from something and want to start afresh or find a new challenge. In any event, you need to regroup. You are flexible enough to change course entirely, and smart enough to learn from your experiences and plan next steps wisely.

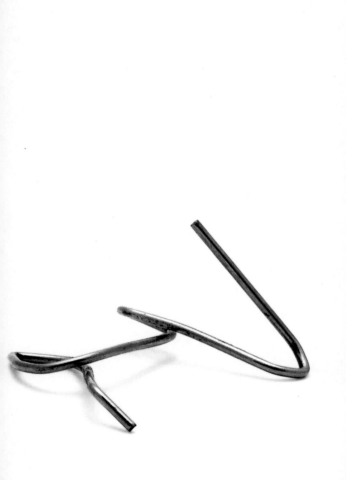

23

You look onwards and upwards with a strong sense of purpose and clarity. Personal enrichment is not your motive: you are committed to the common good. Most of the time you put yourself on a level with others but you like to be able to survey your surroundings. Despite your expansiveness and energy, you move at a measured, deliberate pace. Working proficiently and without fuss, you earn the trust of those around you. They see you as a natural leader and let you take control.

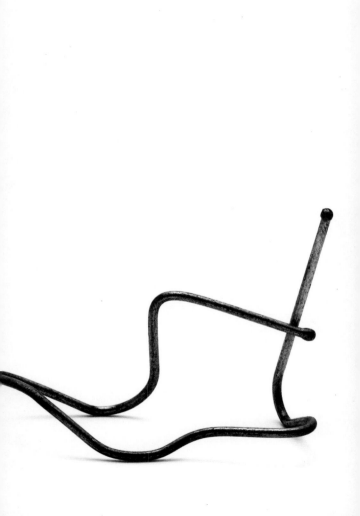

24

You look inwards, seeking the richness
of life in quiet introspection. Turning your
back on new possibilities, you fix your gaze
demonstratively on the past. You keep
your thoughts and experiences to yourself,
storing them inside you like minerals in
the ground. Sharing is not your thing.
You believe sobriety is the route to salvation
and in nipping disorder in the bud.

25

You are trusting, unassuming and open-hearted. You do not cut yourself off from the world and you have nothing to hide. You leave your doors unlocked and your windows open: you do not fear thieves. You are a natural and spontaneous host who makes everyone feel welcome.
You prefer not to draw attention to your accomplishments. You celebrate living rather than achieving.

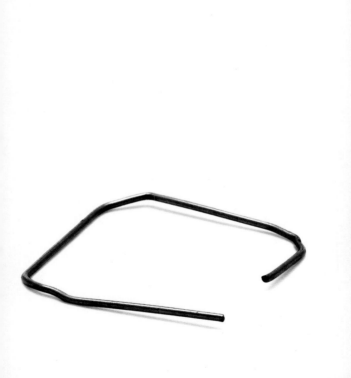

26

You have won great battles and look confidently to the future. Your imposing manner and appearance command immediate respect. Fearing nothing and no one, you push forward to new victories: your natural optimism and past achievements give you strength. You like to maintain a clear overview of any situation but your obvious robustness is protection enough.

27

Your thoughts are geared towards the future. You want to move forward; but at the same time, you feel uncomfortable about pursuing your ambitions too directly or single-mindedly and instead of accelerating you brake or reverse. Your ideas are ambitious and worthwhile but you lack confidence and allow yourself to be thrown off course. You are constantly at risk of losing momentum and plunging into a morass of self-doubt.

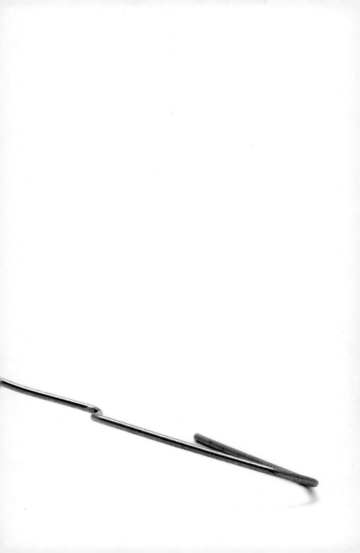

28

You are completely wrapped up in yourself. You brood and pore over things constantly. You sound out your feelings thoroughly before you decide to reveal them – which mostly you don't. When you finally overcome your reservations and put forward a suggestion, it always attracts attention and your proposals are usually taken up. You are a thoughtful and dependable worker, if somewhat lacking in dynamism.

29

You know how to combine practicality and beauty in harmonious, appealing ways. Highly intelligent, you are attuned to form and procedure but you also have a talent for frippery and fun. You set high standards and expect the same from others. Power does not interest you: you value craftsmanship, skill, imagination and ideas.

30

You are a person of many talents, but you hide your light under a bushel. You never hesitate to use your gifts for a worthy purpose and your achievements are impressive, but you prefer to work quietly in the wings. You are self-sufficient and forge your own path. Because of your modesty, you rarely encounter envy, resistance or competition.

31

You look others straight in the eye. You have no problem telling everyone that your friendships are not exclusive and there is room in your life for more. You see no need to choose between rivals: you prefer the infinite possibilities of 'and' to the constraints of 'either ... or'. A peacemaker, you reconcile differences and reunite warring parties. Others would find it exhausting, but you never flag.

32

You do not strive to climb just the highest
peak: you set your sights even higher than
that. Rather than concern yourself with
merely this planet, you reach for the stars.
You are boundlessly ambitious and aim
for the very top. Nevertheless, you manage
to maintain a good grip on reality,
which prevents you from fatal falls.

33

You prefer to hang back and let others solve your problems. Then, when all possible obstacles have been removed from your path, you finally start to stir. You never turn down offers of assistance and would rather sit in the passenger seat than take the wheel. You never seize the initiative: while others lead the way, you tag along with the crowd. If sedan chairs were still around, you would no doubt find a team of porters to carry you about.

34

You are an interloper and like to investigate hidden places and dark crannies. Your inquisitiveness makes you a born explorer but you draw the line at snooping around other people's homes. Despite your curiosity, you generally respect the privacy of those around you. Sometimes your expeditions lead to genuinely valuable discoveries. Your meticulousness is balanced by a generosity of spirit.

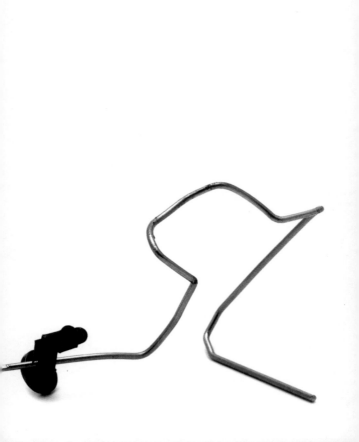

35

You feel the urge to explore. The great
outdoors supplies you with endless
opportunities for pursuing your interest in
arts and crafts. Sometimes you like to stay
put for a while, and you could build a
home from practically nothing. In lean
years you have the skills and aptitude to
live frugally. A survivor who enjoys life and
thinks creatively, you are well equipped
to handle adversity. People tend to wish
you well.

36

You might appear to be fast asleep, but anyone who tries to sneak up on you is making a big mistake. You are ferocious when provoked. Without warning you can bring down unsuspecting intruders and inflict lasting wounds. Like a guard dog that bites before it barks, you leap into action and attack from behind. The best idea is to leave you in peace.

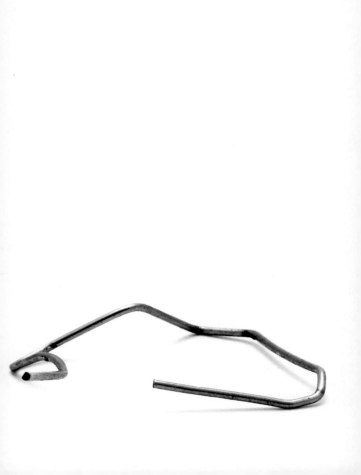

37

You live your own life and make
few demands on the outside world.
Relishing your own company, you seldom
open up enough to let others get close.
Your self-containment means you rarely
make enemies, as you never trespass into
other people's space. You can usually be
found alone or with carefully selected
friends. It could be shyness or perhaps
high expectations that discourage you
from making new connections.

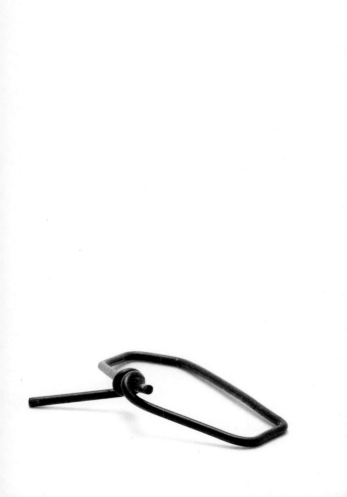

38

You are the golden child, everybody's darling, and you bask in this glow. People do not resent you for your vanity and pride. They see you as the charming girl-next-door, or the perfect son-in-law. You have the strength and poise to assert yourself when necessary, and the whole world is at your feet. Occasionally you are criticised for being smug, but most of the time you can do no wrong.

39

You tire quickly and generally feel run-down. Afflicted by endless problems or ailments, you like to take restorative breaks and tend to back out of social arrangements. Nonetheless, you take a lively interest in what is happening in your absence, and you want to be part of things. Solitude and isolation do not suit you. If an occasion is big enough, you are almost guaranteed to be there, although perhaps not on time. In fact, you underestimate your strength: if you could free yourself from your real or imagined complications the world would be your oyster.

40

You prefer to work with a partner: it means
that someone has always got your back
and makes you feel stronger. Besides, you
would rather not carry the full weight of
responsibility – and it suits you to spread
confusion about who to blame in case
your schemes go wrong. You distract your
victims through cunning and sleight of
hand, then rob them blind. A bank account
in Switzerland or the Caymans would be
helpful to stash your stolen bounty. Once
the deed is done, you disappear without
trace – in search of a new target.

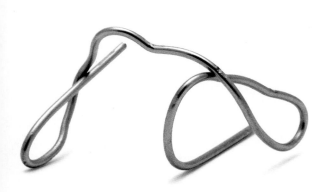

41

You do not wish to rise above others; you like to dwell among peaceful plains and shaded valleys. In your eyes, the still waters of a lake are more appealing than the towering summits of snow-clad mountains. But you are drawn to other people's secrets and the pleasure you take in quiet contemplation also has a darker side. You like to eavesdrop and snoop, whether for the thrill of it or because you stand to gain. You would make an excellent informant for office gossips – or the secret service.

42

You have tremendous clarity of vision and your actions are generous and graceful. You love sweeping designs, bold lines and expansiveness. You do not get lost in details or bogged down by unnecessary concerns. Your love of beauty is matched by your practical grasp of what is needed. With minimal effort you transform your surroundings, which come to bear your trademark style. You do not lean on other people but find peace and balance within.

43

You are nimble and respond quickly to new developments, but you are constantly on the lookout for danger and flee at the slightest hint of a threat. You have the pace and agility to throw off your pursuers, and your deep-seated distrust allows you to see them coming from a distance – unless blind panic has already set in. Despite your natural inquisitiveness and energy, you struggle to muster the courage to venture beyond your familiar environment or embark on new adventures and can often be found at home. You are wary of anything new or unknown.

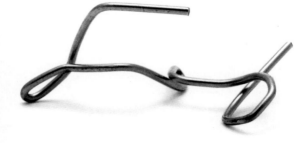

44

You are highly respected. People look up to you and pay attention to what you say. Outwardly, you seem self-assured and easy-going, but you lack the courage to follow your convictions, preferring to wait until things are heading in the right direction before taking the plunge.
You see yourself as unsuited to front-line duty: managing supplies at base camp is more your style. You are what could be called a successful minimalist: you share in people's triumphs without putting in much effort or hard graft of your own.

45

You are not afraid when things get messy
or even chaotic. With your extraordinary
reserves of strength and endurance,
you do not simply weather the storm –
instead you put your all into driving it back.
Your defensive tactics can be indelicate
and unusually forthright: you are prepared
to bring out the heavy artillery if needed.
You do whatever it takes, and your
courage is beyond question.

46

Faced with a challenge you are unflinching. You respond defensively but defiantly: you return every blow without tiring. In a deadlock you refuse to back down and your look of steely determination is usually enough to keep attackers at bay. You defend your fortress tenaciously and stick to your guns. You never revisit old territory and your sights are fixed firmly ahead. With your considerable reserves of energy and mental ammunition you have good cause to be confident of victory but most of the time you can trust in your intimidating appearance to scare off your foes.

47

A love of aesthetic harmony and sensual indulgence characterises your outlook, decisions and artistic work. Nothing you do ever seems forced: you achieve perfection effortlessly. Your ideas flow freely and your creativity is limitless. No one begrudges your success because your talents appear to be genuine. You simply fascinate. You seem half human, half divine; real and yet unearthly – completely beyond reproach. Your seductive power is mighty, but you do not abuse it.

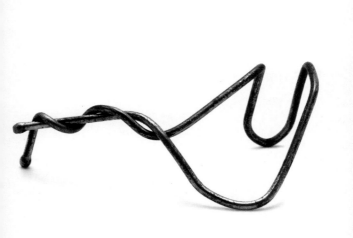

48

You clearly want to succeed – but you are happy not to rush. Although purposeful in your direction, you allow yourself to stop and make detours, approaching your goal without haste. You are not inclined to put on a show for others or pretend to be something you are not. Your expectations are modest: more than anything, you like to be left in peace. Mild-mannered and non-confrontational, you do not aspire to dizzy social or professional heights. You never protest when others push ahead of you: sooner or later you get there regardless – and in your view, the journey is what counts. People may think you are passive, unmotivated or a bit of a lame duck. You do not take offence.

49

Nothing would induce you to roll up your
sleeves, and you are certainly not in
danger of overstraining yourself. You make
life as comfortable as possible – an art form
that you have mastered. Your innermost
thoughts and feelings are kept well hidden:
you might be trying to shut out the outside
world or you could be protecting yourself –
even your motivation remains unclear.
You avoid any form of exertion or activity,
preferring a quiet life without unnecessary
upheaval or stress. In your opinion,
less is always more. You have plenty
of inner space.

50

You do not seek out company. You have
found safe ground and like to be alone.
Proud and aloof, you tend towards
intransigence and stick firmly to your
principles, preferring what you know.
You resist passing fashions and your
steadfastness and intellectual superiority
are respected and admired. People come
to you, not the other way round. Nothing
shatters your composure. You could be
marched away by armed officials and
still maintain your poise. You are majestic
yet robust, a stranger to doubt. Pomposity
and pretension leave you cold.

51

You are rarely in the thick of things.
In fact, you make a point of hanging
back. It is no secret that you do not like
risks and you would rather wait and see.
People think of you as anxious, cautious
and generally conservative. Content
to maintain the status quo, you are
not tempted to chase the latest trend.
Nevertheless, you follow developments
keenly with your own agenda in mind,
waiting until you are doubly – or triply –
certain that the time is right. Eventually
you catch up with the others and
overtake those who jumped the gun.

52

You do not see the fun of creating things: you simply want to own them. Possession is your goal. You like to acquire the achievements of others and stockpile them for yourself. You may be prepared to allow trusted parties access to your collection, but you keep it strictly guarded. Your ambitions are more about quantity than quality and you feel responsible for ensuring that the present does not disappear without a trace. You probably need someone to catalogue your growing archive before it overwhelms you. Be careful not to disappear beneath the clutter.

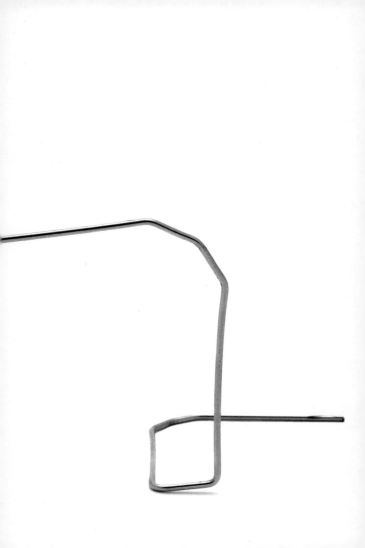

53

You always take the easy way out,
sometimes making a point of it so people
get the message. You live in the moment
as far as possible. Often late, you miss out
on opportunities but your laid-back attitude
means you do not complain or feel
resentment. Zero growth is fine as far
as you're concerned. Provided you
can relax, you are content.

54

You are quick to take charge, give orders and lead the way. You would rather supervise proceedings than do the grafting, and you have no qualms about putting your subordinates to work. You let the project gather momentum, bring yourself up to speed and take the wheel. Whether conducting an orchestra, managing a building site, heading up a business or directing the traffic, you are entirely at ease in leadership roles. Most people trust you because you are naturally authoritative but far from tyrannical. When direction is needed, they look to you.

55

Motivated, determined and dependable, you are the sort of person that everyone wants to have around. You work hard and with integrity to achieve your goals. Moving step by step, you tick off each stage until you reach the top. Before you start working on the next task, you make sure that the current one is watertight. Fair-minded and polite, you would not dream of stealing other people's glory or claiming their achievements as your own. You are committed to self-improvement.

56

You do not aspire to fame, fortune or
higher intellectual planes: you seek
physical passion and sensual pleasure.
Your external needs are modest: enough
space to lie down is all you ask. Wrapped
up in your amorous entanglements, you
shut yourself off from the outside world.
The prospect of romance thrills you. You
have a tendency towards introversion and
to stick your head in the sand, which can
lead you to lose sight of reality. Luxuriating
in the pleasure of the moment can make
you miss important deadlines, and let
valuable opportunities pass you by.

57

Full of natural exuberance, you skip
through life – at times a little too carelessly.
You are sociable, energetic and outgoing,
and you love a bit of small talk. You fit in
anywhere and with anyone, happy to
jump on the bandwagon. Easy-going and
generous in your interactions, you meet
new people all the time. You don't weigh
up your words before you speak and
you are not pedantic. Your propensity
to change your mind and mood can
make people see you as a bit flighty.
You are prone to emotional lows as
well as soaring highs.

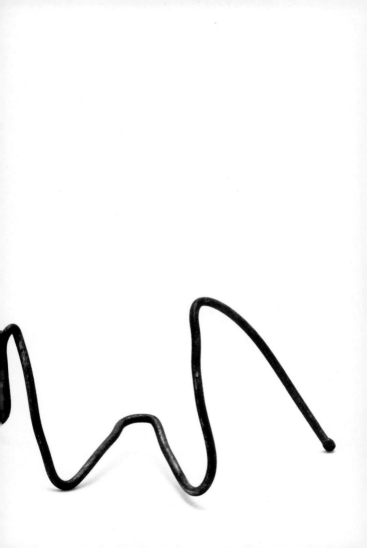

58

You are a warrior through and through.
You take on the most ruthless aggressors
and bring them down. With your strength,
agility and speed, you do not need to call
in reinforcements: you settle the matter
single-handedly, knocking out opponents
in a few deadly moves. Your dominance
over the ground is equalled only by your
mastery of the skies, and your inner
reserves of ammunition are inexhaustible.
Old adversaries will have nothing more to
do with you, but you may be a useful friend.

59

You like to stick with things as they are, only making changes when absolutely necessary. You respect other people and their work, and you do not seek to impose your creative vision or plans. It does not occur to you to adapt existing objects and use them for new purposes: you see value in their intended function and original design. Appearances are not important to you, and you have little time for purely ornamental features. Simple shapes appeal more to you than complex figures, and decorative flourishes arouse suspicion.

60

You want to get to the very top – and the quicker the better. You are not prepared to hang around or wait your turn: your aim is to achieve your ambitions without effort or delay. You have no patience with the maxim that good things come to those who wait. Gain without pain is your goal, and you see pause for thought as wasted time. You feel most comfortable when top of the heap, but you do not seek to step on other people or order them around. Power is not your motivation: you like the view from the top, and no one can touch you.

personality test

If you want to learn more about yourself, this test is for you.

Part 1: Your Individual Personality Profile

1. Take out your test sheet.

2. Turn to the front of the sheet, where you will find pictures of all sixty paperclips featured in this book. There are fifteen rows in total, with four different paperclips in each. Look at the first row and decide which of the four paperclips you like best and appeals to you the most. Put a tick in the corresponding box. Now do the same for the remaining rows. Then turn over the sheet and enter the **numbers** (not the sequence of letters) of your chosen paperclips in the **red column** of

Table 1, beginning with your favourite from the first row and working down. You can set aside the table until Part 2.

3. Next you need to narrow down your fifteen favourites to just three. Go back to the front of the sheet and select your most favourite from the five you ticked in Group A, another from Group B and a third from Group C. Put a circle around your three top favourites.

4. Which of your three favourites speaks to you the most? Enter the **numbers** of your chosen paperclips in order of preference in the **orange boxes** (1–3) of **Table 2** on the back of the sheet. For example, if 22 is your overall favourite, write 22 in the first orange box.

5. Now turn to the main section of this book (pages 13–136) and read the descriptions corresponding to your three favourite paperclips, starting with your first choice, followed by your second and third. These descriptions make up the first part of **your personality profile**.

Part 2a: Supplementary Test

1. Turn to the back of the test sheet. The supplementary test shows fourteen pairs of paperclips. Look at the first pair. Which paperclip do you prefer? Stick with your immediate response and tick the corresponding box marked 'V' or 'W'. Now pick your favourite from the second pair, and so forth.

2. How many 'V's and how many 'W's have you selected? Count them up and enter the totals in the boxes provided. You will need the results for the next part of the test: your typological profile.

Part 2b: Your Typological Profile

1. On the front of the test sheet you will see a series of letters beneath each paperclip. Look at the **red column** in **Table 1** where you wrote the numbers of your fifteen favourite paperclips. Go through the first row of the table and tick all the letters printed beneath your chosen paperclip.

Let's suppose you entered paperclip 2 in the first row. Printed beside the paperclip are the letters B, G, K and M, so you should tick these letters. To save turning the sheet every time, note down the letters for each of your fifteen favourites on a notepad before transferring the results to the table.

2. Now go to the orange boxes in **Table 2** where you wrote the numbers of your top three paperclips and write down the corresponding **letters** in the **blue boxes**.

3. Return to **Table 1** and count up the number of ticks for each letter. Write the totals in the **brown boxes** at the bottom of each column.

4. The letter columns in **Table 1** are grouped into neighbouring pairs. Looking at the totals for each pair of columns (AB, CD, EF, etc.), subtract the smaller total from the larger total for each pair and enter the result in the corresponding **yellow box** at the bottom of the table. For example, if column 'E' has a total of 8 and column 'F' has a total of 12, your calculation would look like this: 12 – 8 = 4.

5. To complete your **typological profile** you need to fill in the **purple** and **pink** boxes as follows:

a. Look at the yellow boxes at the bottom of **Table 1** where you recorded the difference between each pair of letters AB, CD, EF, GH and IK. If the number in the yellow box is **five or more**, go back to the brown boxes with the total for each letter and find out which letter in the pair had the greater number of ticks. Now write that letter in the **purple box**. For example: if you have a five in your yellow box for AB, you should check your brown boxes for A and B. Let's suppose you have a seven in Box A and a two in Box B. The number in Box A is greater than Box B, so write the letter A in your purple results box.

b. Now focus on the yellow boxes for columns LM, NO and PQ. If the number in each box is **four or more**, go back to the brown boxes in the row above, find out which letter in the pair had the greater number of ticks, and add the letter to the **purple box**. For example: if you have a five in the yellow box for LM, you need to check your brown boxes for L and M. Let's suppose you have a seven in Box L and a three in Box M. The number in Box L is greater than Box M, so include the letter L in your purple results box.

c. Look at the number in the yellow box for column RS. Is it **three or more**? If so, go back to the brown boxes, check whether R or S had more ticks, then add that letter to the **purple box**.

d. Now look at the purple box. If there are **two or more** letters, then add a 'T'. If there are no letters, enter a 'U'. If there is a single letter, don't add anything.

e. Go back to the blue boxes where you wrote the letters corresponding to your top three paperclips. If a single letter appears in all three rows, write that letter in the **pink box** to the right. For example, if you find an 'A' among the letters in each of the three blue rows, you should include the letter 'A' in your pink results box. If none of your letters appear in all three rows, you should leave the pink box blank and go straight to step 5h. Otherwise continue to 5f.

f. Focus again on the purple box. Does it contain one or more of the following letters: A, D, F, H, I, L, O, P, R or V? If so, check the pink box to see whether it contains the other letter from that particular pair. For example, if you find an 'A' in your purple box, you should check your pink box for a 'B'. If you find a paired letter in the pink box, write 'X1' in the **purple box**.

g. Now look at the pink box. Does it contain one or more of the following letters: A, D, F, H, I, L, O, P, R or V? If so, check the purple box to see whether it contains the other letter from that particular pair. If you find a paired letter in the purple box, write 'X2' in the **purple box**.

h. Turn to the results of the supplementary test from Part 2a. If the number in your 'V' box is eleven or more, add a 'V' to your **purple box**. If the number in your 'W' box is eleven or more, add a 'W' instead. If you have six, seven or eight in either your 'V' or your 'W' box, you should enter 'VW' in your **purple box**; otherwise proceed to the final stage.

i. Transfer all the letters in the purple and pink boxes to the large empty box on the right. Congratulations: these are your results! In the next section of the book you can look up the descriptions corresponding to your letters and put together your typological profile. Some letters may appear more than once in your results box: simply cross out any repetitions.

typological

profile

ambitious

You intend to succeed. You want to rise to the top and be admired by others, indeed perhaps be in charge of them too.

b

modest

You are undemanding. You do not aspire to power or fame: maybe you lack self-confidence – or maybe you are simply comfortable as you are.

C

conservative/sceptical

You worry all the time. You approach anything new or different with scepticism, you stay out of danger, and you dislike adventures or risk. Reserved and unforthcoming, you are mistrustful of others, keeping your distance or shutting them out entirely.

d

progressive/open-hearted

You love a challenge. You are optimistic about the future and approach situations energetically. You have no trouble trusting other people; you are generous in your interactions, welcoming everyone, even strangers, with open arms.

primitive

You have a tendency to be boorish
and coarse, and don't always
manage to strike the right tone.

f

cultivated

You have a very sensitive, sophisticated, cultured and generally distinguished character. You set high aesthetic standards and you fulfil them.

traditional

You avoid change wherever possible and wish for everything to remain the same.

h

metamorphic

You make sweeping changes without hesitation. You are happy to throw out the old to make room for the new.

robust

You are not intimidated by difficult, complicated or fraught situations. You rise to all challenges – you may even enjoy them.

fair

You dislike chaos, confusion and messiness. You want things to be clear, open and upfront.

I

regal/energetic

You are strong, robust and resilient. You find positive solutions to problems and have plenty of stamina. Dignity and self-possession are important to you; you cultivate inner calm and like to maintain a broad overview. You aren't interested in petty rivalries and power struggles. Most of the time you enjoy being above it all.

asthenic/subordinate

You tend to be fragile, powerless and timid. You tire quickly, you are often clumsy and careless, lack a strong will, and generally need protection and support. You rely on having a solid roof over your head.

n

phlegmatic

You are easy-going and enjoy things. Nothing gets you in a flap, and you seldom lose your cool. You stay calm, take your time and like to relax.

active

You are bursting with energy,
dynamic and quick to act.
You get things moving.

hostile

You are rancorous, resentful and antagonistic. You tend to compete with others and sometimes come to blows. Everyone is a potential enemy for you.

q

amicable

You are well disposed towards others.
You respect their achievements,
never begrudge them their success
and you are happy to help
when you can.

elegant

You express your feelings, desires and frustrations in brilliant, elegant and playful ways, whether in how you communicate with others or in creative and artistic pursuits.

s

primal

You do not always have the ability or concentration to channel your emotions and desires in ways that other people accept or expect. Your analysis of situations lacks nuance and your responses are simplistic. This may be a result of your present circumstances or your current frame of mind.

homogenous

You are consistent and dependable
in your preferences; you know what
you want. You may be somewhat
one-sided or blinkered in your opinions,
but you know your own mind.

u

heterogeneous

You have varied tastes, you are
open to new experiences and
are flexible in your outlook.

V

affective

You wear your heart on your sleeve and express your feelings openly or even effusively – perhaps excessively so. Colour plays an important role for you: you seek to make dark or drab environments blossom. This could be your way of banishing boredom or shutting out negative thoughts.

rational

You approach most things logically and objectively and tend to keep your feelings in check. You like things to be systematic and orderly. The uncertainty of emotions makes you nervous.

affective/rational

You usually maintain a balance between emotion and logic. You express your feelings adequately and you are able to integrate them into your judgements and decisions. Consequently your opinions and positions seem reasonable and fair.

x1

non-completing

You embark on things energetically, enthusiastically and sometimes daringly, but when it comes to the crunch you tend to reconsider, modify your original position or even take a step backwards, reverting to existing patterns, possibly because you doubt yourself and take fright.

x2

late-starting

You approach things hesitantly and circumspectly, exercising caution and hanging back. In time – or at the very last minute – you opt for ambitious, progressive, modern or even radical solutions and innovations, sometimes to the astonishment of those around.

x1 x2

mutable

You tend to change your mind –
sometimes at the last minute and
completely without warning.
All of a sudden you hit the brakes
and go into reverse, or you defy
expectations by taking a giant leap
forward. No one can be sure of your
vote until you leave the ballot box.

Paperclip Index

The names relate to the paperclips as works of art. The titles are not part of your personality profile!

Are you missing the test sheet or would you like to do the test again?

You can print out extra copies from
www.thepapercliptest.com